INTRODUCTION

Welcome back to FastTrack®!

Hope you enjoyed *Guitar 1* and are ready to play some hits. Have you and your friends formed a band? Or do you feel like soloing with the CD? Either way, make sure you're turned up loud…it's time to jam!

With the knowledge you already have, you're ready to play all of these eight songs. But it's still important to remember the three Ps: **patience**, **practice** and **pace yourself**.

As with *Guitar 1*, don't try to bite off more than you can chew. If your fingers hurt, take some time off. If you get frustrated, put down your guitar, relax and just listen to the CD. If you forget a chord or note position, go back and learn it. If you're doing fine, think about charging admission.

CONTENTS

ABOUT THE CD

Again, you get a CD with the book! Each song in the book is included on the CD, so you can hear how it sounds and play along when you're ready.

Each example on the CD is preceded by one measure of "clicks" to indicate the tempo and meter. Pan right to hear the guitar part emphasized. Pan left to hear the accompaniment emphasized.

HAL•LEONARD®
CORPORATION
7777 W. BLUEMOUND RD. P.O. BOX 13819 MILWAUKEE, WI 53213

Visit Hal Leonard Online at
www.halleonard.com

LEARN SOMETHING NEW EACH DAY

We know you're eager to play, but first you need to learn a few new things. We'll make it brief—only two pages…

Melody and Lyrics

All of the melody lines and lyrics of these great songs (except "Walk Don't Run" which is an instrumental) are included for your musical pleasure (and benefit). These are shown on an extra musical staff, which we added above your part.

Sometimes you will be playing this melody, too. Other times you're supporting this melody with chords. Either way, you can easily follow the song as you play your part.

And whether you have a singer in the band or decide to carry the tune yourself, this new staff is your key to adding some vocals to your tunes.

New Chords

In addition to the nine chords you learned in *Guitar 1*, one of the songs contains some new chords. Here they are in notation, tablature, and diagrams. They're easy but require practice.

"Walk Don't Run"

Smack 'em a few times to get the feel…

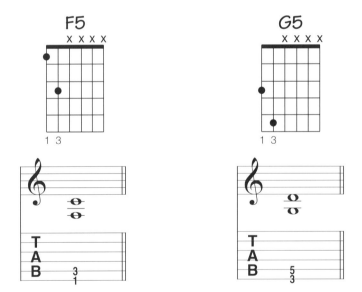

NOTE: The song "Evil Ways" has an E7 chord. Forget it: your part is just an E5 power chord. Similarly, "Jailhouse Rock" has the chords C7, D7, and G7. Nevermind the "7"—you just play C, D, and G, chords you already know.

Endings

Several of the songs have some interesting little symbols that you must understand before playing. Each of these symbols represents a different type of **ending**.

1st, 2nd, and 3rd Endings

These are indicated by brackets and numbers:

Simply play the song through to the first ending, then repeat back to the first repeat sign, or beginning of the song (whichever is the case). Play through the song again, but skip the first ending and play the second ending.

Two songs, "Gimme Some Lovin" and "Jailhouse Rock," have a **3rd ending**. But this is really the same principle as a 2nd ending—just one more repeat and ending for one more terrific melody.

D.S. al Coda

When you see these words, go back and repeat from this symbol: 𝄋

Play until you see the words *"to Coda"* then skip to the Coda, indicated by this symbol: 𝄌

Now just finish the song.

Song Structure

Most songs have different sections, which might be recognizable by any or all of the following:

 INTRODUCTION (or "intro"): This is a short section at the beginning that (you guessed it again!) "introduces" the song to the listeners.

 VERSES: One of the main sections of the song is the **verse**. There will usually be several verses, all with the same music but each with different lyrics.

 CHORUS: Perhaps the most memorable section of a song is the **chorus**. Again, there may be several choruses, but each chorus will often have the same lyrics and music.

 BRIDGE: This section makes a transition from one part of a song to the next. For example, you may find a bridge between the chorus and next verse.

 SOLOS: Sometimes solos are played over the verse or chorus structure, but in some songs the solo section has its own structure. This is your time to shine!

 OUTRO: Similar to the "intro," this section brings the song to an end.

That's about it! Enjoy the music...

Evil Ways

Words and Music by Sonny Henry

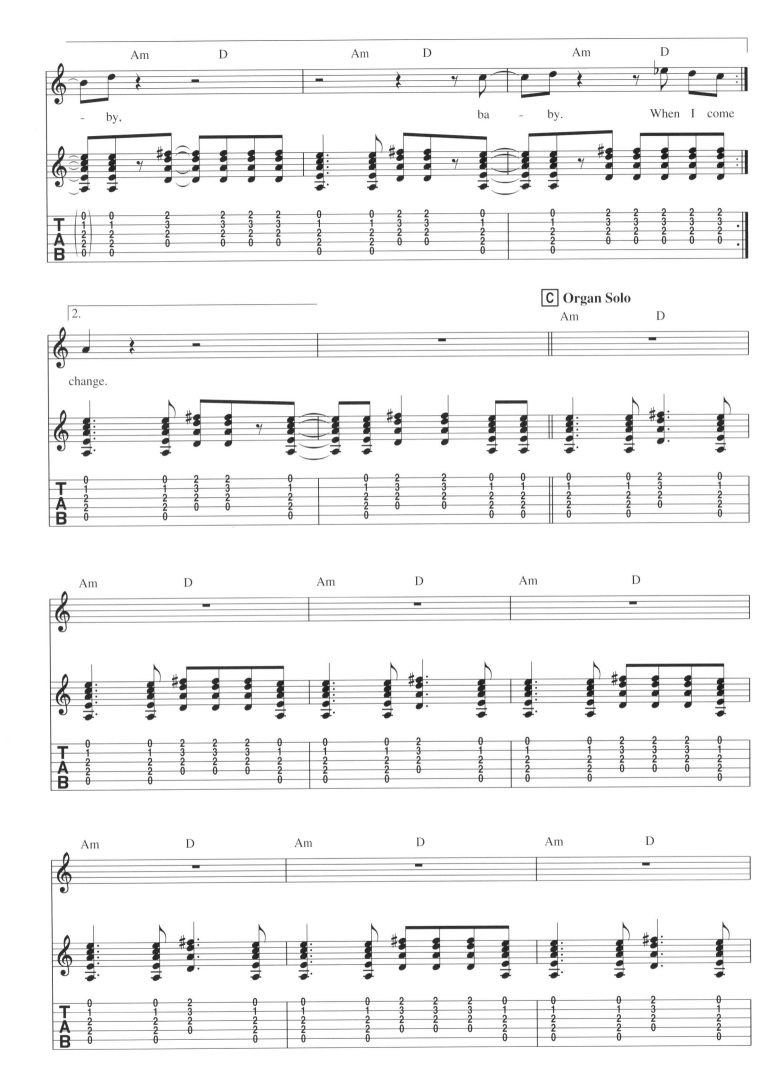

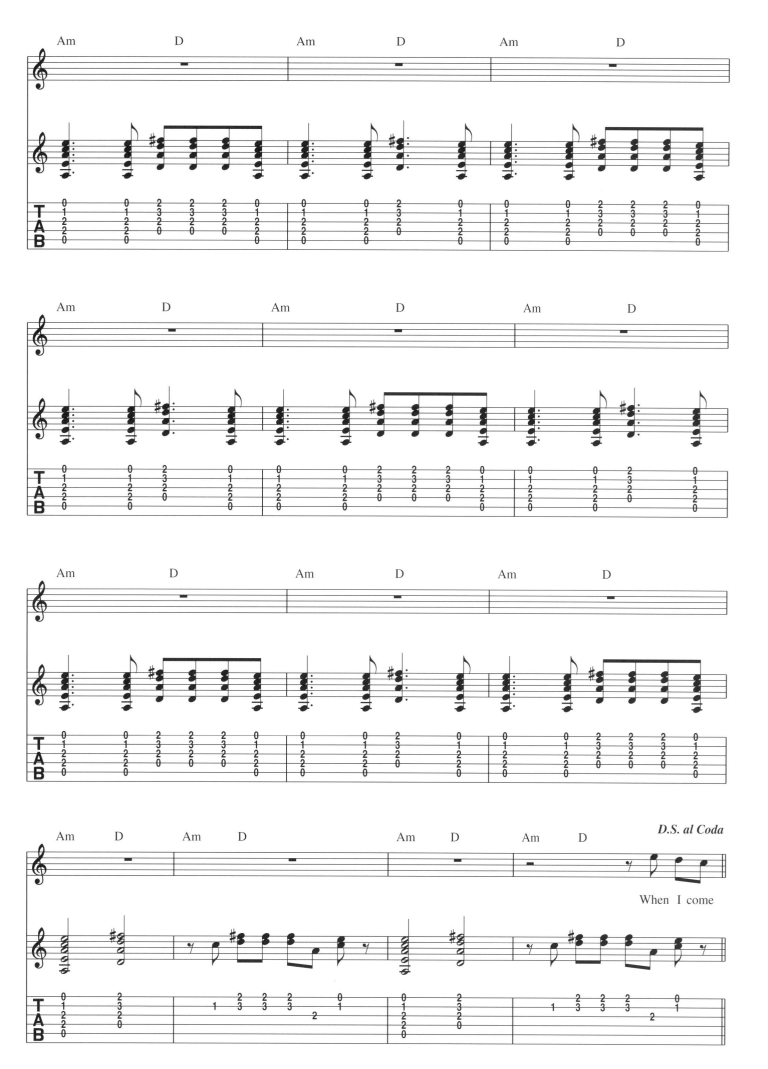

D.S. al Coda

When I come

Gimme Some Lovin'

Words and Music by Spencer Davis, Muff Winwood and Steve Winwood

A Intro

Moderately Fast ♩ = 152

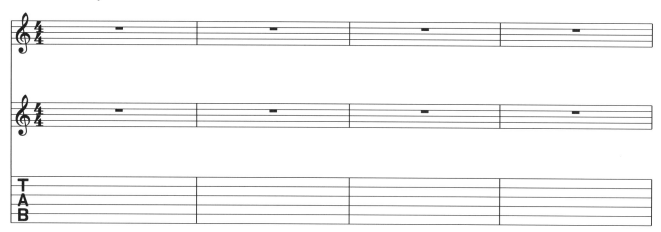

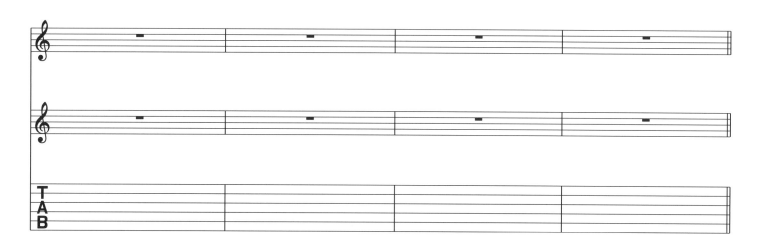

B Interlude

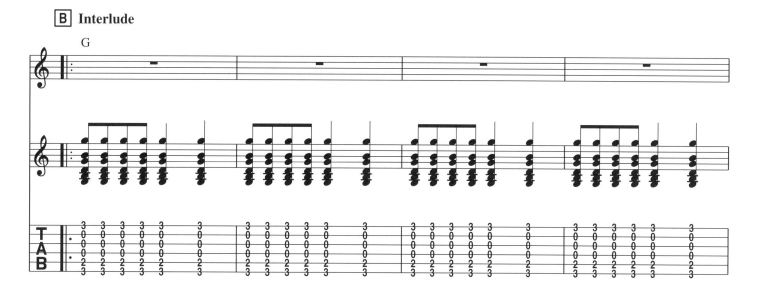

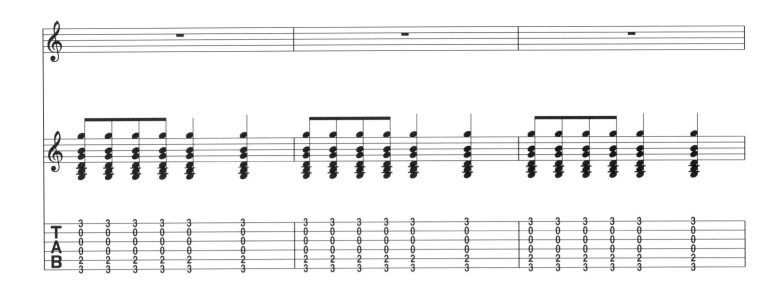

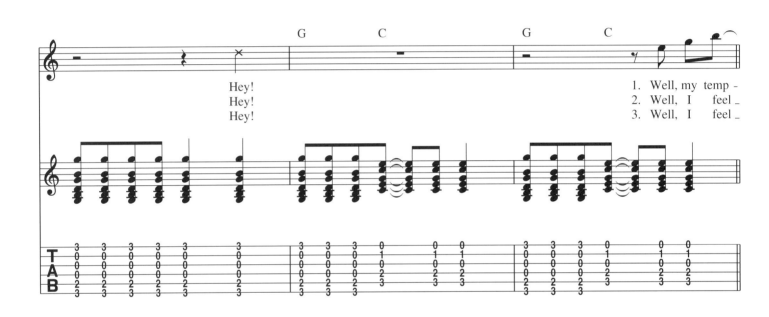

C Verse

11

(Gim-me gim-me some lov - in'.) Gim-me some __ a lov-in'. Ev - 'ry day. __

(Gim-me, gim-me some lov - in'.)

(Gim-me, gim-me some lov - in'.)

Gloria

Words and Music by Van Morrison

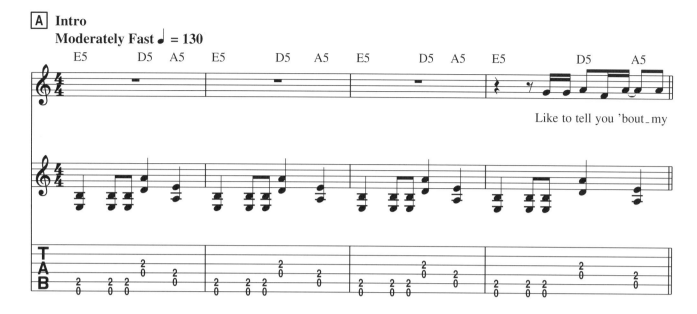

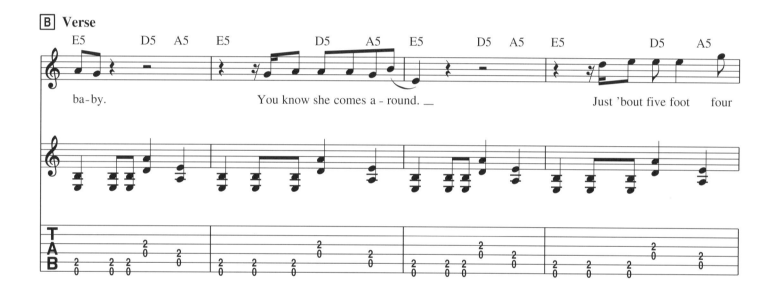

She comes a - round

◆4 Have I Told You Lately

Words and Music by Van Morrison

Have I told you late-ly that I love you? Have I

told you there's no one else a-bove _ you? Fill my heart _ with glad-ness,

take a-way all _ my sad-ness, ease my trou-bles that's _ what you do. For the

C **Verse**

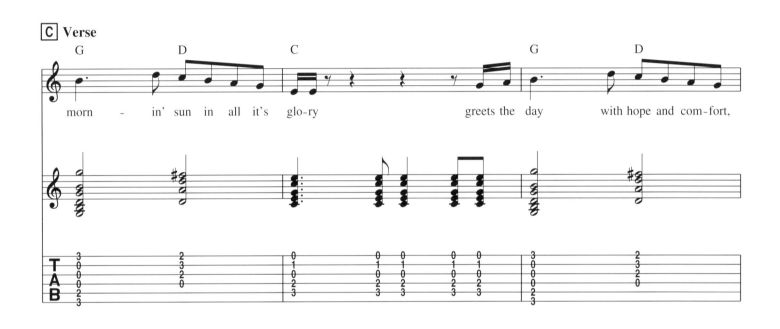

morn - in' sun in all it's glo-ry greets the day with hope and com-fort,

too. You fill my life with laugh-ter and some-how you make it bet - ter,

ease my trou-bles that's _ what you do.   There's a love that's di-vine,

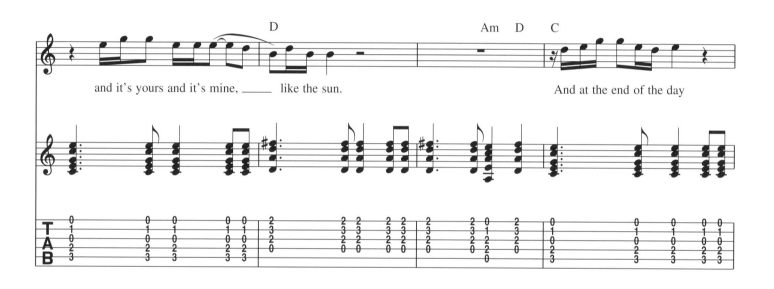

and it's yours and it's mine, _____ like the sun.   And at the end of the day

we should give thanks and pray ____ to the one, _   to the one. _   Have I

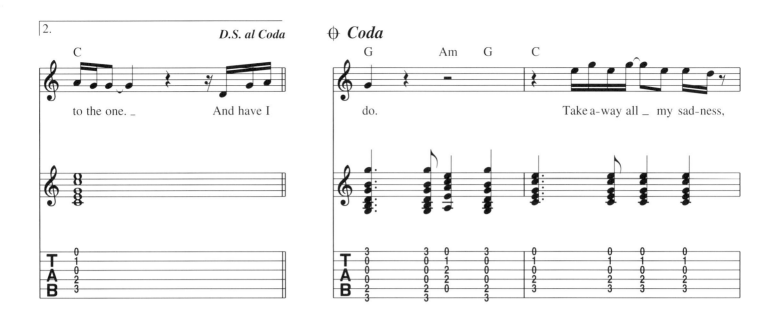

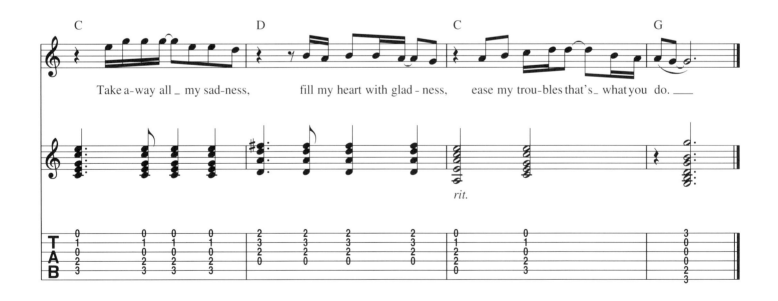

Jailhouse Rock

Words and Music by Jerry Leiber and Mike Stoller

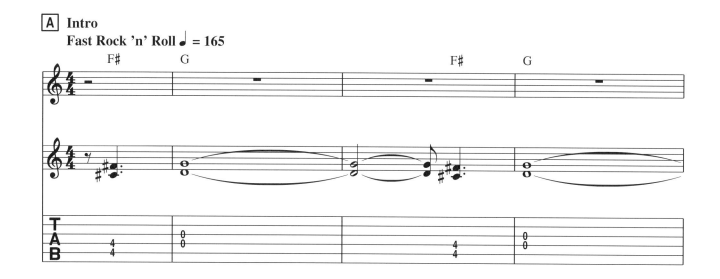

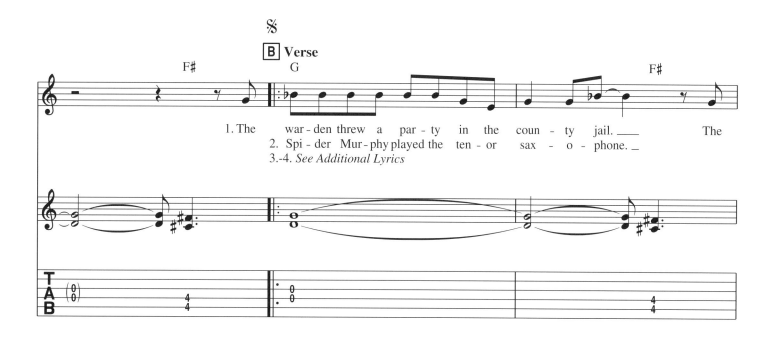

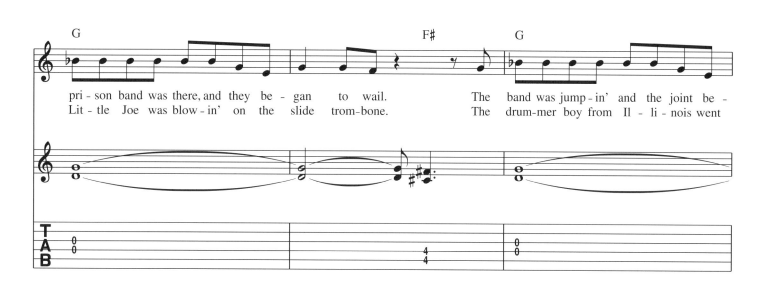

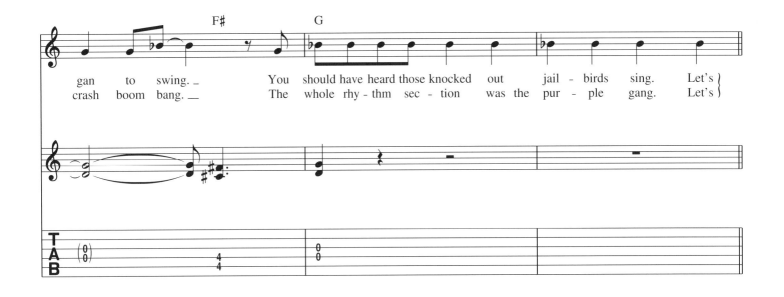

gan   to   swing. __   You   should have heard those knocked   out   jail - birds   sing.   Let's
crash   boom   bang. __   The   whole rhy - thm   sec - tion   was the   pur - ple   gang.   Let's

C Chorus

rock!   Ev - 'ry - bod - y, let's   rock!

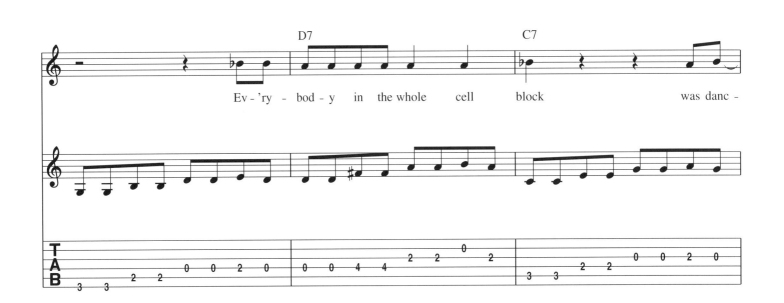

Ev - 'ry - bod - y   in   the whole   cell   block   was danc -

ing to the Jail - house Rock! Rock!

D **Guitar Solo**

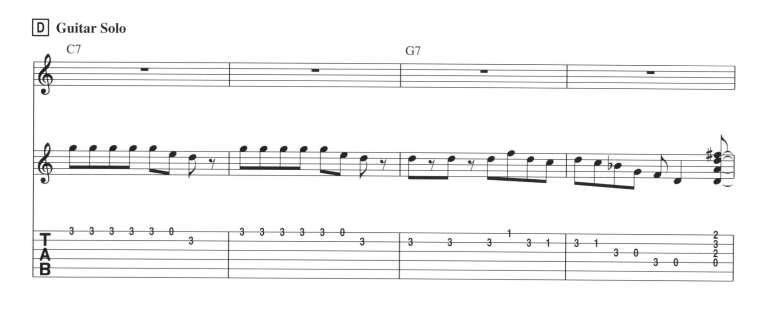

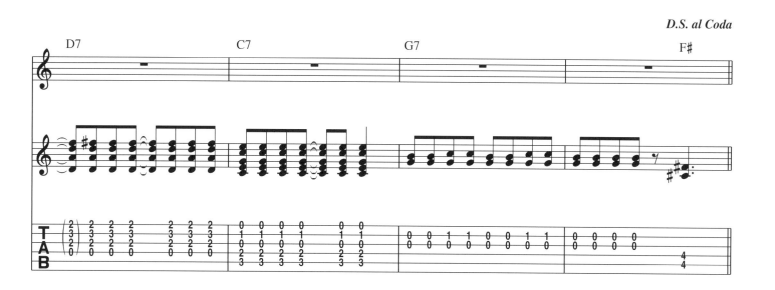

Rock! Danc - ing to the Jail - house Rock! Danc - ing to the Jail - house

Rock!

Additional Lyrics

3. Number Forty-seven said to number Three:
   "You're the cutest jailbird I ever did see.
   I sure would be delighted with your company.
   Come on and do the Jailhouse Rock with me."

4. The sad sack was a-sittin' on a block of stone,
   Way over in a corner weeping all alone.
   The warden said: "Hey, Buddy, don't you be no square,
   If you can't find a partner, use a wooden chair!"

   (optional)

5. Shifty Henry said to Bugs: "For heaven's sake.
   No one's lookin', now's our chance to make a break."
   Bugsy turned to Shifty and he said, "Nix, nix;
   I wanna stick around a while and get my kicks."

Time Is on My Side

Words and Music by Jerry Ragovoy

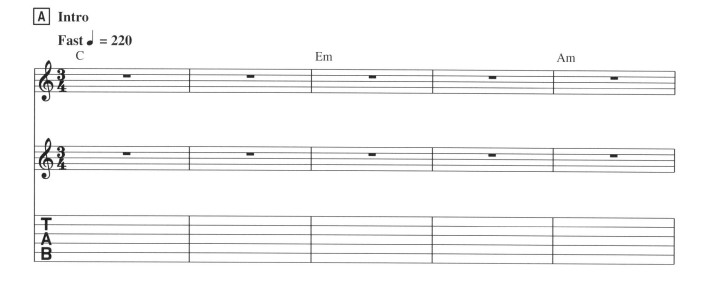

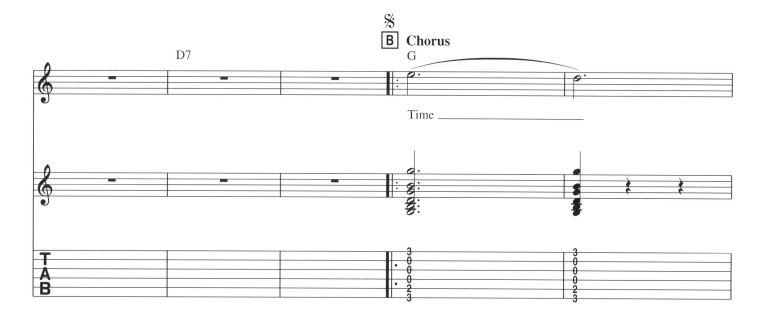

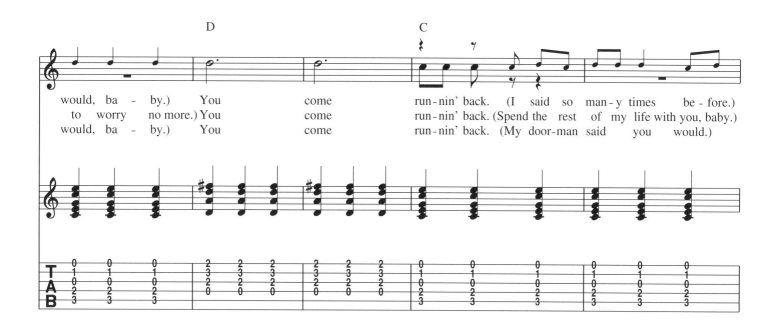

would, ba - by.) You come run-nin' back. (I said so man - y times be - fore.)
to worry no more.) You come run-nin' back. (Spend the rest of my life with you, baby.)
would, ba - by.) You come run-nin' back. (My door-man said you would.)

You'd come run - nin' back to me. _____
You'll come run - nin' back to me. _____
You'd come run - nin' back to me. _____

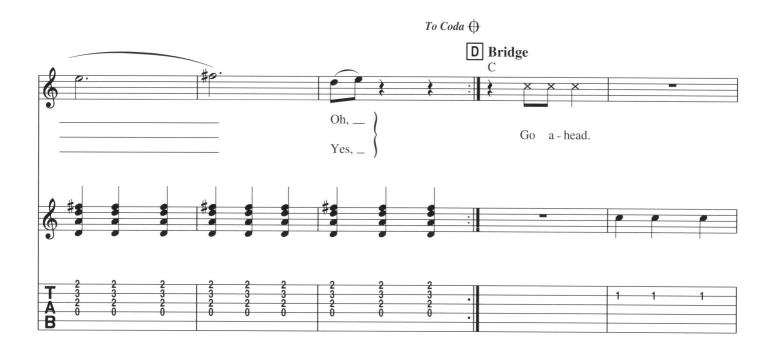

To Coda ⊕

D **Bridge**

Oh, __
Yes, __

Go a - head.

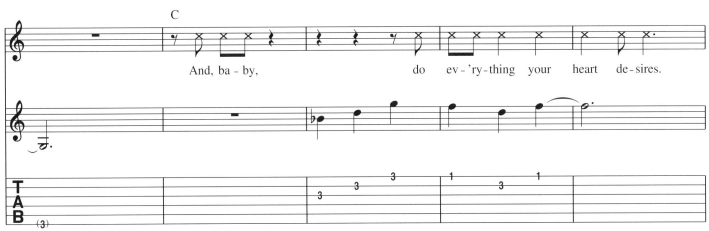

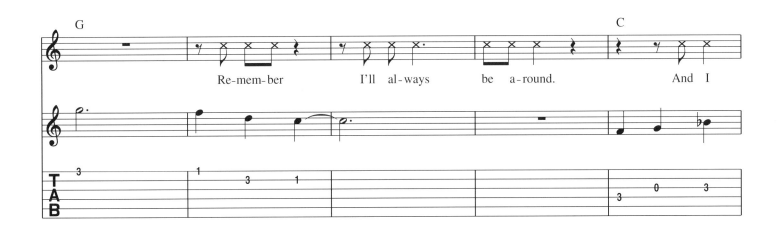

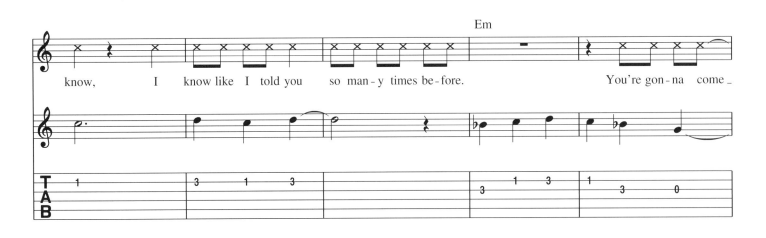

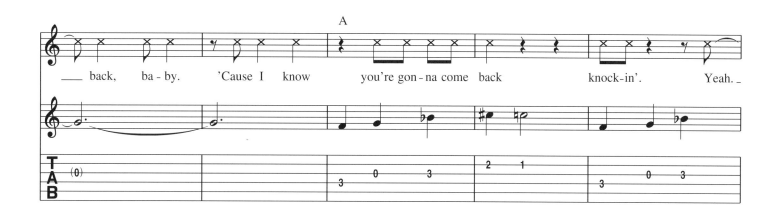

_back, ba - by. 'Cause I know you're gon - na come back knock-in'. Yeah. _

D.S. al Coda

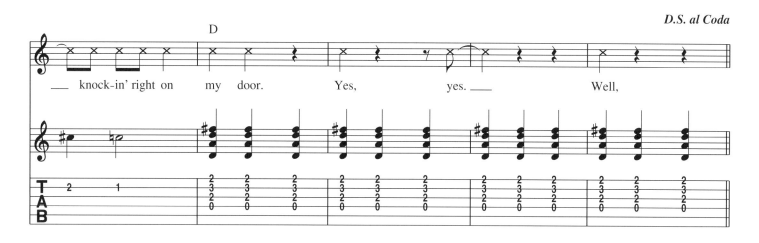

_ knock-in' right on my door. Yes, yes. _ Well,

⊕ *Coda*

E **Outro-Chorus**

Time, time, time is on my _ side. _

1., 2.   3.

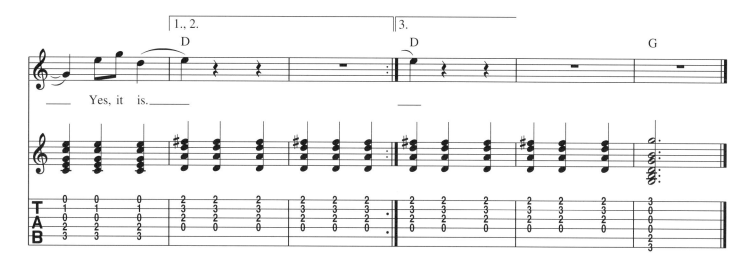

_ Yes, it is. _

31

7 Twist and Shout

Words and Music by Bert Russell and Phil Medley

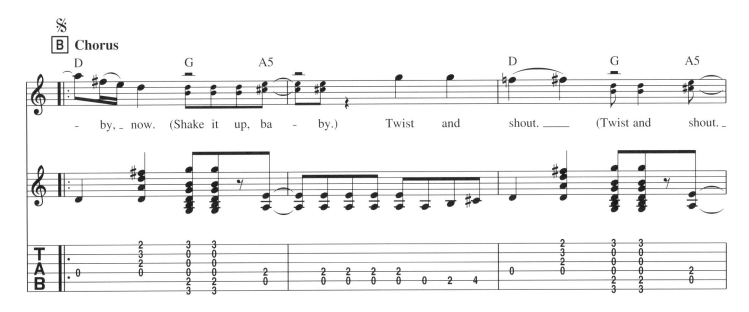

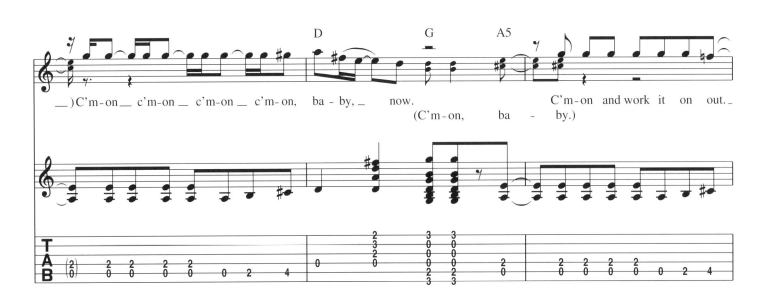

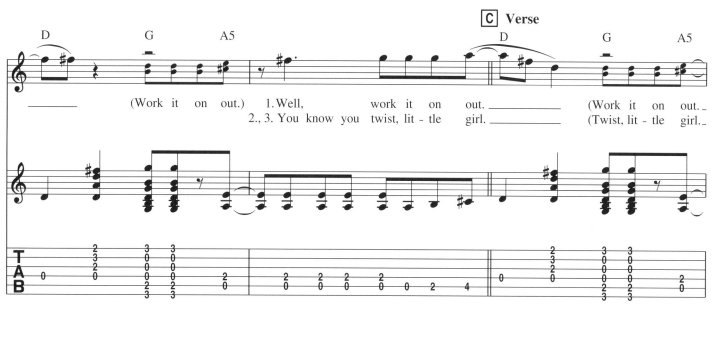

(Work it on out.) 1. Well, work it on out. _____ (Work it on out. ___
2., 3. You know you twist, lit - tle girl. _____ (Twist, lit - tle girl. _

___) You know you look so good. (Look so good. ___) You know you got me
___) You know you twist so fine. (Twist so fine. ___) C'm - on and twist a lit - tle

go - in' ___ now. (Got me go - in'.) Just like I knew ___ you would. ___ (Like I knew you would.)
clos - er ___ now. (Twist a lit - tle clos - er.) And let me know ___ that you're mine. (Let me know you're mine.)

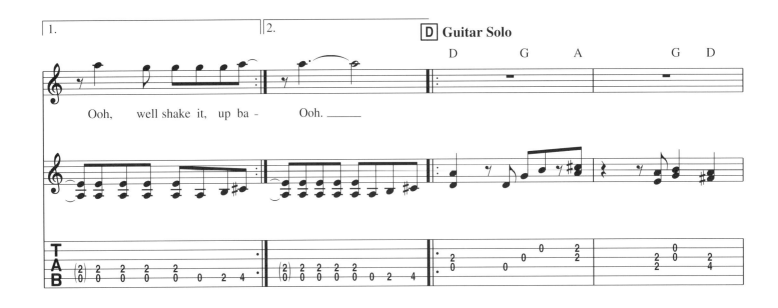

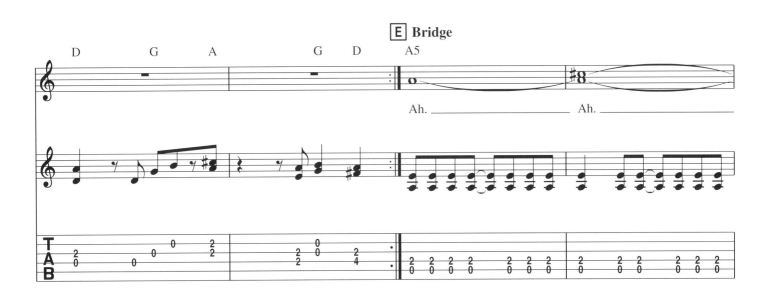

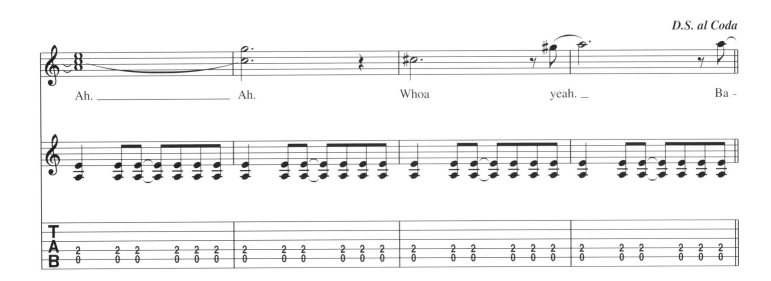

Well, shake it, shake it, shake it, ba - by, __ now.   Well, shake it, shake it, shake it,
(Shake it up, ba - by.)

ba - by, __ now.   Well, shake it, shake it, shake it, ba - by, __ now.
(Shake it up, ba - by.)   (Shake it up, ba - by.)

F **Outro**

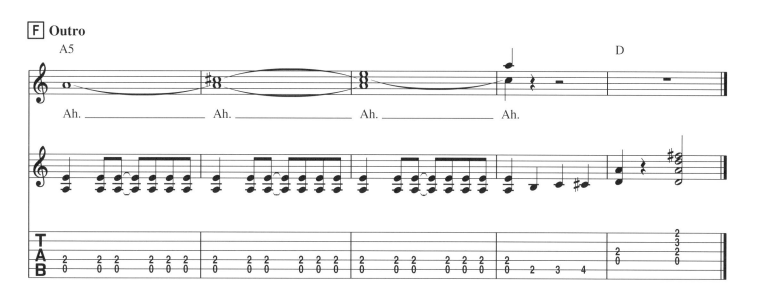

Ah. _____ Ah. _____ Ah. _____ Ah.

Walk Don't Run

Words and Music by Johnny Smith

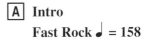

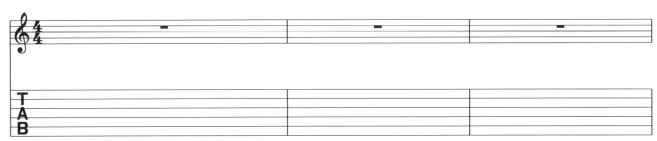

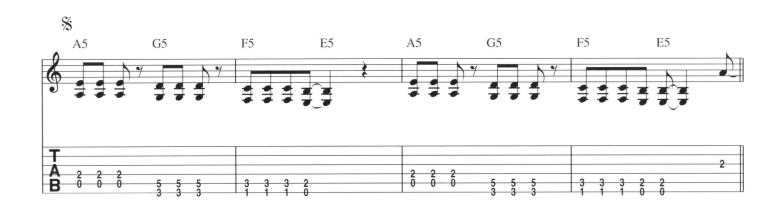

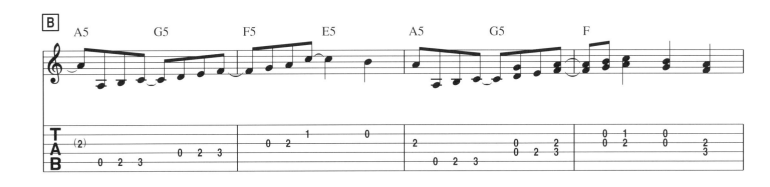

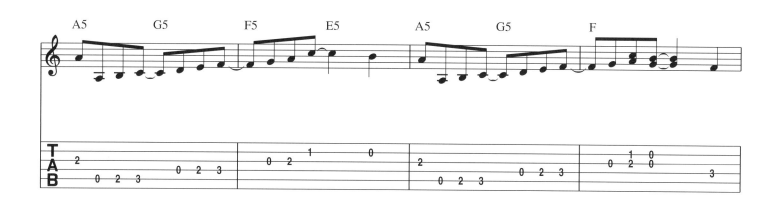

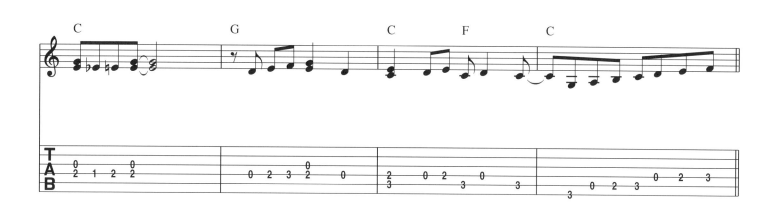

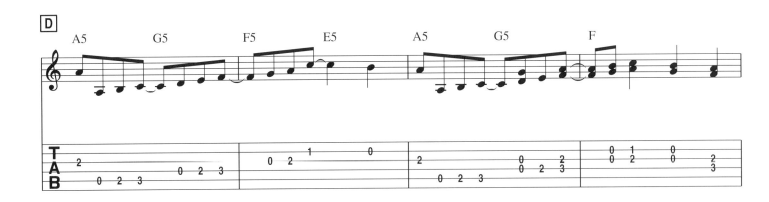

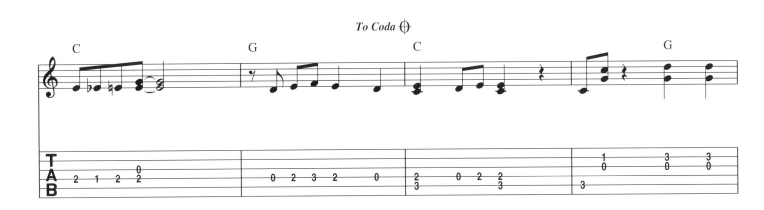

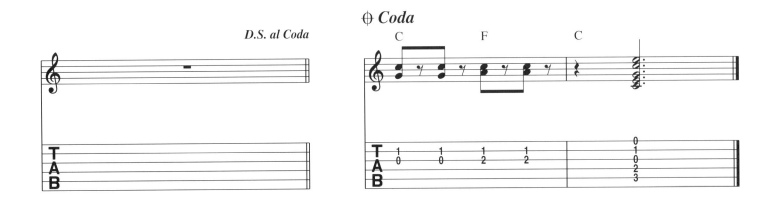

FastTrack™
MUSIC INSTRUCTION

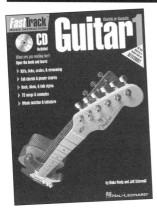

*Fast*Track is the fastest way for beginners to learn to play the instrument they just bought. *Fast*Track is different from other method books: we've made them user-friendly with plenty of cool songs that make it easy and fun for players to teach themselves. Plus, the last section of the *Fast*Track books have the same songs so that students can form a band and jam together. Songbooks for Guitar, Bass, Keyboard, and Drums are also compatible, and feature eight songs including hits like Wild Thing, Twist and Shout, Layla, Born to Be Wild, and more! All packs include a great play-along CD with professional-sounding back-up band.

*FAST*TRACK GUITAR

For Electric or Acoustic Guitar – or both!
by Blake Neely & Jeff Schroedl
Teaches music notation, tablature, full chords and power chords, riffs, licks, and scales, and rock and blues styles. Method Book 1 includes 73 songs and examples.

METHOD BOOK 1
00697282 Book/CD Pack.......................................$7.95

SONGBOOK 1 – LEVEL 1
00697287 Book/CD Pack.....................................$12.95

SONGBOOK 2 – LEVEL 1
00695343 Book/CD Pack.....................................$12.95

CHORDS & SCALES
00697291 Book/CD Pack.......................................$9.95

METHOD BOOK 2
00697286 Book/CD Pack.......................................$9.95

SONGBOOK 1 – LEVEL 2
00697296 Book/CD Pack.....................................$12.95

SONGBOOK 2 – LEVEL 2
00695344 Book/CD Pack.....................................$12.95

*FAST*TRACK BASS

by Blake Neely & Jeff Schroedl
Everything you need to know about playing the bass, including music notation, tablature, riffs, licks, and scales, syncopation, and rock and blues styles. Method Book 1 includes 75 songs and examples.

METHOD BOOK 1
00697284 Book/CD Pack.......................................$7.95

SONGBOOK 1 – LEVEL 1
00697289 Book/CD Pack.....................................$12.95

SONGBOOK 2 – LEVEL 1
00695368 Book/CD Pack.....................................$12.95

METHOD BOOK 2
00697294 Book/CD Pack.......................................$9.95

SONGBOOK LEVEL 2
00697298 Book/CD Pack.....................................$12.95

*FAST*TRACK KEYBOARD

For Electric Keyboard, Synthesizer, or Piano
by Blake Neely & Gary Meisner
Learn how to play that piano today. With this book you'll learn music notation, chords, riffs, licks and scales, syncopation, and rock and blues styles. Method Book 1 includes over 87 songs and examples.

METHOD BOOK 1
00697283 Book/CD Pack.......................................$7.95

SONGBOOK 1 – LEVEL 1
00697288 Book/CD Pack.....................................$12.95

SONGBOOK 2 – LEVEL 1
00695366 Book/CD Pack.....................................$12.95

CHORDS & SCALES
00697292 Book/CD Pack.......................................$9.95

METHOD BOOK 2
00697293 Book/CD Pack.......................................$9.95

SONGBOOK LEVEL 2
00697297 Book/CD Pack.....................................$12.95

*FAST*TRACK SAXOPHONE

by Blake Neely
With this book, you'll learn music notation; riffs, scales, keys; syncopation; rock and blues styles; and includes 72 songs and examples.

METHOD BOOK 1
00695241 Book/CD Pack.......................................$7.95

SONGBOOK 1 – LEVEL 1
00695409 Book/CD Pack.....................................$12.95

*FAST*TRACK DRUM

by Blake Neely & Rick Mattingly
With this book, you'll learn music notation, riffs and licks, syncopation, rock, blues and funk styles, and improvisation. Method Book 1 includes over 75 songs and examples.

METHOD BOOK 1
00697285 Book/CD Pack.......................................$7.95

SONGBOOK 1 – LEVEL 1
00697290 Book/CD Pack.....................................$12.95

SONGBOOK 2 – LEVEL 1
00695367 Book/CD Pack.....................................$12.95

METHOD BOOK TWO
00697295 Book/CD Pack.......................................$9.95

SONGBOOK LEVEL 2
00697299 Book/CD Pack.....................................$12.95

*FAST*TRACK HARMONICA

by Blake Neely & Doug Downing
These books have all you need to learn C Diatonic harmonica, including music notation, singles notes and chords, riffs, licks and scales, syncopation, rock and blues styles. Method Book 1 includes over 70 songs and examples.

METHOD BOOK 1
00695407 Book/CD Pack.......................................$7.95

SONGBOOK 1 – LEVEL 1
00695411 Book/CD Pack.....................................$12.95

*FAST*TRACK LEAD SINGER

by Blake Neely
Everything you need to be a great singer, including: how to read music, microphone tips, warm-up exercises, ear training, syncopation, and more. Method Book 1 includes 80 songs and examples.

METHOD BOOK 1
00695408 Book/CD Pack.......................................$7.95

SONGBOOK 1 – LEVEL 1
00695410 Book/CD Pack.....................................$12.95

FOR MORE INFORMATION, SEE YOUR LOCAL MUSIC DEALER,
OR WRITE TO:

HAL•LEONARD®
CORPORATION
7777 W. BLUEMOUND RD. P.O. BOX 13819 MILWAUKEE, WI 53213

Prices, contents, and availability subject to change without notice. Some products may not be available outside the U.S.A.

0100